Its Ok Not To Be Okay

Let's Face It Together

E J Marsh

Contents

Preface

At its heart, It's OK Not to Be OK is a message of understanding, compassion, and action—a lifeline for children, parents, educators, and every adult who cares about the well-being of our younger generations. Brought to you by From Darkness to Dawn Publishing, this work is more than just a story; it's a movement, a call to arms, and a deeply human reminder that we all have a role to play in raising awareness and creating safer spaces for our children to grow and thrive.

This book addresses the harsh realities of cyberbullying, a pervasive issue that affects countless children every day. Through storytelling, it shines a light on the importance of open conversations, parental involvement, and a community effort to tackle bullying in all its forms. As a professional body committed to raising awareness through storytelling, From Darkness to Dawn Publishing brings this work to life with the intent of not just educating, but also inspiring action.

The story within these pages is carefully crafted to resonate with children aged 7 to 12 while serving as a powerful resource for adults. It bridges the gap between awareness and understanding, offering both a gripping narrative and practical insights. More than that, it's a mirror that reflects the world we live in—one where challenges like bullying demand collective solutions and empathy-driven action.

This isn't just a book to be read; it's a tool for change. It's a means to spark critical discussions at the dinner table, in classrooms, and within the community. It's a guide for parents unsure of how to approach difficult conversations, and for children who may feel isolated or voiceless. It's an opportunity for educators, social workers, and even law enforcement to see firsthand the profound impact of collective awareness and intervention.

With every page, It's OK Not to Be OK invites readers to step into a story that is all too real for many—and to leave with the courage, tools, and determination to make a difference. Whether you're here as a parent seeking guidance, an educator looking to foster understanding, or a child finding solace in the shared experience of others, this book was written for you.

Our hope is that this story not only touches your heart but ignites a spark of action—one that builds bridges of communication, awareness, and care. Together, we can create a world where no child feels alone in their struggles, and every adult understands the vital role they play in nurturing resilience and kindness. After all, it truly is OK not to be OK—but it's never OK to stay silent in the face of suffering.

Welcome to a book that isn't just about reading—it's about transforming.

E J Marsh

Chapter 1
Shadows Online

Jamie's fingers hover over the tablet screen, the light from the device casting a faint glow on his face. He's not playing games or watching videos like he used to. Instead, he scrolls through the group chat, rereading the same messages over and over.

Kyle:

"You're such a loser ."

Kyle:

"Bet you won't even show your face tomorrow. Scared?"

Kyle: "Everyone knows you're weird. Just stop trying."

Jamie's chest tightens. He doesn't reply—he hasn't for days. Each time he types something, he deletes it before hitting send. No matter what he says, Kyle will twist it into something worse.

The emojis mock him: the laughing faces, the clowns, the thumbs-down. They seem harmless, but they sting more than words ever could.

He wishes he could just leave the group, but he knows the teasing won't stop—it'll only get louder at school. He sets the tablet down and stares at the darkened screen. His reflection stares back, tired and heavy-eyed.

Downstairs, Mum and Dad sit at the kitchen table, their voices low but urgent.

Mum:

"He's barely spoken all week. And have you seen him? He's not eating properly, and he doesn't even touch his football anymore."

Dad:

"I know. I tried talking to him yesterday, but he just shrugged me off. I think something's going on at school—or online. You've seen how glued he is to that tablet, but now it's different. He's not laughing at videos or showing us memes anymore."

Mum:

"What if someone's bullying him? You know how kids are these days—it's not just in the playground anymore. It's everywhere. And the worst part? You can't even see it happening."

Dad exhales sharply, leaning back in his chair. "We need to tread carefully. If we push too hard, he'll shut us out completely. But we can't just stand by, either. Tomorrow, I'll try to sit with him while he's on his tablet. Maybe he'll let something slip."

The next morning, Jamie sits at the dining table, his tablet propped up against a cereal box. His parents watch him closely as he scrolls. The usual chatter of breakfast is replaced by an uneasy quiet.

Mum:

"Jamie, love, what are you looking at?"

He shrugs, not looking up. "Just stuff," he mutters.

Dad leans over slightly. "Can I see?"

Jamie pulls the tablet closer to his chest, his movements sharp and defensive. "It's nothing, okay?"

Mum and Dad exchange a glance. Mum places a gentle hand on Jamie's arm.

Mum:

"You know, if something's bothering you, you can tell us. We're here for you."

Jamie's eyes flicker with something—fear? Shame?—but he doesn't say a word. He pushes his chair back abruptly and leaves the table, his cereal untouched.

That evening, Jamie locks his bedroom door and sinks onto the bed. The tablet sits beside him, its screen lighting up every few seconds with new messages.

Kyle:

"What's wrong? Cat got your tongue? "

Kyle:

"Go on, cry about it. Everyone knows you're too scared to do anything."

Jamie swipes the notifications away, but the words linger in his mind, echoing like a taunt.

He opens the group chat, hesitates, and then types: "Leave me alone."

His thumb hovers over the send button, but he deletes the message before it can go through.

In the quiet of his room, Jamie feels the weight of the shadows creeping in. He hugs his knees to his chest, wondering if tomorrow will be any different—or if it will only get worse.

Downstairs, Mum and Dad sit together, their worry growing heavier with each passing day.

Mum:

"We need to do something. He's shutting us out more and more."

Dad:

"We will. But we have to do it carefully. Tomorrow, let's sit him down together and make sure he knows he doesn't have to face this alone."

As the clock ticks toward midnight, Jamie lies awake in his bed, the tablet's screen dark. But the shadows it casts in his mind are far from gone.

Chapter 2
Behind The Emoji

Jamie sits at the breakfast table, the soft glow of his tablet casting faint shadows on his face. Notifications ping relentlessly, each one a reminder of something he'd rather forget. His fingers hover over the screen, unsure whether to open the messages or turn it off entirely.

His dad walks into the room, coffee mug in hand.

Dad:

"Morning, mate. You're a bit quiet today. Everything alright?"

Jamie doesn't answer. He flips the tablet face-down on the table, his shoulders slumping as he stares at the untouched toast on his plate.

Mum:

"Jamie, love, we've noticed you've not been yourself lately. You're not as chatty as usual. Is something wrong?"

Jamie shrugs, still avoiding eye contact.

Dad:

"Is it something at school? Or... is it online?"

Jamie's lips tighten as another notification chimes. He glances briefly at the screen before looking away, a shadow of worry crossing his face.

Mum:

"If someone's giving you a hard time, you can tell us. We're here to help."

Jamie finally speaks, his voice barely audible.

Jamie:

"It's nothing."

Dad:

"It doesn't seem like nothing, son. You've been on edge for days now. Whatever it is, you don't have to deal with it alone."

Jamie flinches as his dad gestures toward the tablet.

Dad:

"Let's take a look together. We'll figure this out."

Jamie's head snaps up, panic flashing in his eyes. He grabs the tablet and holds it tightly to his chest.

Jamie: "No! You can't look!"

Mum:

"Jamie, sweetheart, we just want to help. Whatever's going on, it's not too big for us to handle together."

Jamie shakes his head, tears welling up in his eyes.

Jamie:

"You don't get it. You can't fix this!"

Before they can say another word, Jamie bolts from the table, the chair scraping loudly against the floor. He dashes upstairs and slams his bedroom door.

Mum:

"Jamie! Please, come back!"

Dad:

"Jamie, wait! We're not angry, we just want to help!"

The sound of the lock clicking echoes down the hallway, leaving Mum and Dad standing in the kitchen, their faces etched with worry.

Mum sits down heavily at the table, her hands trembling.

Mum:

"I've never seen him like this before. He's so scared. What do we do?"

Dad:

"We give him a little space for now. But we can't leave him to deal with this on his own. If he won't talk to us, we'll have to involve someone else—a teacher, maybe a counsellor."

Upstairs, Jamie sits on his bed, staring at the tablet screen. The cruel messages glare back at him, each word cutting deeper than the last. His hands shake as he scrolls through them, the mocking emojis and taunts playing over and over in his mind.

Kyle:

"Can't handle the heat? Maybe just disappear. "

Anonymous:

"What a loser. "Kyle: "Everyone knows. You're pathetic. "

Jamie locks the screen and throws the tablet onto his pillow. He buries his face in his hands, muffling the sound of his sobs.

Downstairs, Mum and Dad exchange worried glances.

Mum:

"Maybe his little sister knows something? Lily's always around him. She might have seen or heard something."

Dad:

"It's worth a try. Let's talk to her."

They find Lily sitting on the living room floor, playing with her toys. She looks up at them with curious eyes.

Mum:

"Lily, can we talk to you for a minute, sweetheart?"

Lily:

"Is Jamie okay? He seemed upset."

Dad:

"That's what we're trying to figure out. Has Jamie said anything to you? Or maybe you've seen him acting differently?"

Lily shakes her head.

Lily:

"He doesn't really talk to me about stuff like that. He says I'm too little."

Mum:

"You're not too little, love. But if you do hear anything or see anything that worries you, promise you'll tell us?"

Lily nods solemnly.

Lily:

"I promise."

Later that evening, Mum and Dad sit together at the dining table, their voices hushed.

Mum:

"If Lily doesn't know anything, maybe Lucas does. Jamie spends more time with him than anyone else."

Dad:

"Good idea. I'll give his mum a call."

An hour later, Lucas arrives at the house with his mum. He sits awkwardly on the couch, fidgeting with the hem of his hoodie.

Dad:

"Thanks for coming, Lucas. We're really worried about Jamie. Has he said anything to you? Or have you noticed anything different at school?"

Lucas shifts uncomfortably, avoiding eye contact.

Lucas:

"No... not really. I mean, he's been a bit quiet, but I don't know what's wrong."

Mum:

"Lucas, we're not angry. We just want to make sure Jamie's okay. If there's something you know, you can tell us."

Lucas hesitates, his hands twisting nervously.

Lucas:

"I... I don't know. He hasn't said anything to me. I wish I could help, but... I really don't know."

Dad:

"Alright, Lucas. Thanks for being honest."

As Lucas leaves, Mum and Dad sit back down at the table, the weight of the situation pressing down on them.

Mum:

"If Lucas doesn't know anything, and Jamie won't talk to us, what do we do?"

Dad:

"We don't stop trying. He needs us, even if he doesn't know how to say it."

Chapter 3 Secrets Shared

Lucas stares at the floor, his hands trembling. He bites his lip, his face pale and drawn.

"I... I don't know, Mr. Carter," he whispers. "I'm sorry."

Jamie's dad leans forward, his voice calm but insistent.

"Lucas, we know you're Jamie's best friend. He's scared, and we're trying to understand why. If there's anything you know, it's really important that you tell us."

Lucas fidgets with the hem of his hoodie, his chest rising and falling with shallow breaths.

"It's... it's complicated," he mutters, barely audible.

Jamie's mum softens her voice.

"Lucas, sweetheart, you're safe here. You can talk to us. Whatever it is, we won't be angry. We just want to help Jamie—and you, if you need it."

Lucas clenches his fists tightly, his knuckles whitening.

"You don't understand," he says, his voice cracking. "I... I can't tell you. I just can't."

Jamie's dad furrows his brow, leaning back slightly. "Lucas, we're not here to get anyone in trouble. But if you don't tell us what's going on, we can't help Jamie—or you."

Lucas's eyes snap up, his lip trembling as tears pool in his eyes. He hesitates, his breathing shaky, before blurting out, "It's not just Jamie."

Jamie's mum exchanges a sharp glance with her husband before leaning closer.

"What do you mean? Lucas, please talk to us."

Lucas hesitates, his voice trembling as he speaks. "It's Brandon... He's been messaging me too."

Jamie's dad sits up straighter, his voice firm.

"Brandon? Who's Brandon?"

Lucas's shoulders slump as tears streak down his cheeks. "He's... he was our friend. But now he's not. He's been telling me to pick on Jamie—saying if I don't, he'll come after me too."

Jamie's mum covers her mouth, her eyes wide. "Oh, Lucas... Why didn't you tell anyone?"

Lucas sobs quietly, wiping his face with his sleeve. "Because Brandon said if I told, he'd ruin me at school. He said no one would believe me anyway. I didn't know what to do."

Jamie's dad places a steady hand on Lucas's shoulder.

"Lucas, listen to me. What Brandon is doing is wrong, and you don't have to deal with this alone. You've been caught in the middle, and that's not fair. We're going to help you—and Jamie. I promise."

Lucas sniffles, nodding slightly.

"But Brandon's not going to stop... He always finds a way."

Jamie's mum takes a deep breath, her voice steady but determined.

"We'll talk to Jamie and go to the school. This isn't something you or Jamie should face alone. You've been very brave for telling us, Lucas.

That's the first step."

The Next Morning

Jamie's parents sit across from Mr. Daniels, his teacher, in a quiet office. Mr. Daniels listens intently, his expression serious as Jamie's mum explains the situation.

"Thank you for bringing this to my attention," Mr. Daniels says, jotting down notes. "Bullying is something we take very seriously. But I need to ask—when did Jamie start showing signs of distress?"

Jamie's dad exchanges a glance with his wife before answering. "It's been a few weeks. He's been withdrawn and quiet at home, which isn't like him. Then last night, Lucas told us Brandon has been sending threatening messages."

Mr. Daniels nods, his pen hovering over his notebook. "Brandon has been in trouble before for disruptive behaviour, but this is the first I've heard of bullying. I'll need to speak with both boys and escalate this to the headteacher immediately."

Jamie's mum leans forward, her voice shaking.

"We're also planning to involve the police. Brandon needs to understand the damage he's causing."

Mr. Daniels sighs, setting his pen down. "I completely understand, Mrs. Carter. But we'll need to follow school protocol first. I assure you, we'll take this seriously."

Later That Afternoon

Jamie and Lucas sit side by side on the couch, their heads low, as Officer Reynolds, a community police officer, speaks calmly.

"This is a difficult situation," he says, looking between the boys and their parents. "Since everyone involved is a minor, we can't press charges. However, we can collaborate with the school and involve a social worker to ensure this stops."

Jamie looks up, his voice barely a whisper. "But what if Brandon finds out? He won't stop. And what if his brother gets involved?"

Officer Reynolds raises an eyebrow.

"Brandon has an older brother?"

Lucas nods hesitantly. "Yeah... Kyle. He's worse. He doesn't like it when Brandon gets in trouble. If he finds out, he'll go after Jamie—or me."

Jamie's mum gasps softly, covering her mouth, while Jamie's dad clenches his jaw.

"Are you saying this goes beyond just Brandon?" he asks.

Lucas nods again, his voice shaky. "Yeah... Kyle's always hanging around the school gates. He's not someone you mess with."

Officer Reynolds scribbles in his notebook.

"Thank you for telling me this. I'll include it in my report. In the meantime, it's important for you both to keep speaking up. You're not alone in this."

Jamie glances at Lucas, who offers him a small, nervous smile. Jamie nods, his voice trembling but resolute. "Okay. We'll keep talking."

Chapter 4
The Cyber-storm

A week later, Jamie and Lucas walk home from school, their steps slow, their eyes darting to every shadow. The sun hangs low in the sky, casting long shadows over the pavement.

At the corner, Kyle steps out from behind a parked car. His arms are crossed, his smirk smug, and his eyes narrow with malice.

"Well, well," Kyle sneers sarcastically. "My little brother causing trouble, yet again? And now you both think running to mommy and the police is going to fix everything? "

Jamie freezes. His breath catches in his throat as his heart pounds in his chest.

Lucas shifts uncomfortably, stammering, "Kyle, we didn't—"

"Save it, grass" Kyle interrupts, his voice sharp and cutting.

He steps closer, his posture looming.

"You think grassing will stop this? You're just making it worse for yourselves."

Jamie grabs Lucas's arm. His voice is shaky, but he tries to sound brave.

"Let's go, Lucas. He's not worth it."

Kyle blocks their path with a single step, his smirk fading into a dark scowl. Without warning, he swings his fist, connecting with Lucas's nose. The sickening crunch echoes through the quiet street.

Lucas stumbles back, clutching his face as blood trickles between his fingers. His eyes are wide with pain and fear.

Kyle glares down at them.

"What, you thought this was over? How wrong are you? This is just the beginning."

Jamie steps between Kyle and Lucas, his voice trembling but determined.

"Stop it, Kyle! You've already hurt him. Just leave us alone."

Kyle's jaw tightens as he stares Jamie down, his expression unreadable. Finally, he spits out, "Stay out of it. This doesn't concern you."

He glares at Lucas one last time, then steps back.

As he turns to walk away, he delivers one final threat.

"Don't be grassing again to anyone, or it'll just get worse for you."

Jamie kneels beside Lucas, his voice soft and full of worry. "Lucas, are you okay? We need to get you some help."

Lucas nods weakly, his hands trembling as he wipes at the blood on his face. But his eyes stay fixed on the ground, the weight of Kyle's threat pressing down on him.

That night, Lucas sits alone in his room. The door is closed, the lights are off, and the air feels heavy. His tablet rests beside him, its screen dark, but the messages from Kyle replay in his mind like a broken record.

His chest tightens with each memory, each cruel word, each impossible demand. He glances toward the hallway, imagining his parents laughing in the kitchen, oblivious to the storm raging inside him.

If only I'd told them sooner... Maybe this wouldn't have happened. But now it's too late. They wouldn't understand. They'd just get angry—or worse, disappointed.

His eyes drift to the bathroom door. He knows what's inside—the little bottle in the medicine cabinet. He closes his eyes, the thought clawing at him, relentless and unforgiving.

The next morning, the quiet of Lucas's home shatters with a scream.

After his mother casually enters his room, her face begins to pale as she finds him slumped on the bed, unresponsive. The empty pill bottle lies next to him, a stark reminder of his silent suffering.

Jamie's parents carry and rush him outside as an ambulance pulls up outside, its flashing lights illuminating the quiet street in shades of blue and red.

Paramedics move quickly, lifting Lucas onto a stretcher. Although is face pale, his breaths shallow but steady.

Jamie stands in the doorway, his fists clenched at his sides, tears streaming down his face. His mother rests a hand on his shoulder, but he barely feels it. His gaze stays fixed on his best friend as the stretcher disappears into the back of the ambulance.

"Lucas... why?" Jamie whispers, his voice breaking.

He grips his mother's hand tightly, the question hanging heavy in the air.

Chapter 5
The Quiet Storm

At the hospital, the emergency room buzzes with controlled chaos. Doctors and nurses move with purpose, their voices calm yet urgent.

Lucas lies unconscious, pale against the stark white of the hospital bed. Monitors beep steadily, a fragile reassurance of life still holding on.

In the waiting room, Lucas's parents sit huddled together, their hands tightly clasped.

Their faces are etched with exhaustion and fear, shadows of the sleepless night they've endured. Jamie's parents sit beside them, quiet pillars of support, their presence a silent reminder that they're not alone in this.

Hours pass, each one dragging like an eternity, before a doctor finally approaches. Her scrubs are wrinkled, and there's a gentle weariness in her eyes.

"Lucas is stable," she says softly. "He'll need time to recover, both physically and emotionally. It's going to be a journey, but he's going to be okay."

Relief washes over Lucas's parents, but it's fragile, like glass ready to shatter at the slightest touch. Jamie's mum squeezes Lucas's mother's hand, whispering,

"He's strong. He'll get through this."

Later that day, the air in Lucas's living room feels heavy, like a storm that hasn't quite passed. The social worker and police officer sit across from Lucas's parents, their expressions professional yet compassionate. Jamie's parents linger nearby, their faces drawn with concern.

The police officer speaks first, his voice measured and steady.

"We've reviewed the situation. While no charges will be brought at this time, we need to ensure everyone involved is safe moving forward. This isn't just about Lucas—it's about creating a safe environment for everyone."

Lucas's mother nods, her hands trembling.

"We just want him to be okay. He's our baby. We never thought..." Her voice falters, breaking under the weight of guilt and fear.

The social worker leans forward, her tone kind but firm.

"Lucas's well-being is our priority. That includes ensuring his home is a safe space. I understand the medication was accessible in your bedroom. It's crucial to keep items like that secured, especially now."

Lucas's father rubs his hands over his face, the lines of worry deepening.

"We've always kept it out of reach. We never imagined he'd... we didn't think—" He stops, unable to finish the sentence.

"These situations are incredibly difficult," the social worker says gently. "But they also provide an opportunity to make things better. We'll work with you to ensure Lucas has the emotional and mental support he needs. This will include counselling and possibly support groups."

The police officer clears his throat, his gaze steady. "We've also spoken to Kyle's parents. They've been made aware of the severity of the situation. We'll monitor closely to ensure it doesn't escalate further. However, our priority is ensuring Lucas—and others—remain safe."

Lucas's mother looks at the social worker, her voice barely above a whisper. "What happens next?"

The social worker offers a reassuring nod. "We'll arrange regular check-ins to ensure Lucas's recovery and safety. This will be a collaborative effort between your family, the school, and other resources."

As the officer and social worker prepare to leave, Jamie, who has been quietly listening, suddenly speaks up. His voice is small but determined.

"What about Kyle?" he asks, his eyes filled with both fear and defiance.

"Will he stop hurting people now?"

Jamie's father places a steady hand on his son's shoulder, his voice firm yet gentle.

"That's what this is about, Jamie—making sure it never happens again."

Jamie nods slowly, the weight of those words settling over him. But as the door closes behind the officer and social worker, he can't help but wonder if the storm has truly passed—or if it's only just beginning.

Chapter 6 Broken Connections

The house feels different now. Quieter. Heavier. As if the walls themselves are holding onto the weight of what happened.

Jamie sits at the kitchen table, his fingers curled around a mug of lukewarm tea, staring out of the window at the rain tapping against the glass.

His dad's words echo in his head:

"That's what this is about—making sure it'll never happen again."

Lucas is home, but nothing feels normal—not yet.

Jamie catches glimpses of him—sitting alone in his room, walking slowly down the hallway, his gaze distant.

There's a shadow in Lucas's eyes, a quiet weight that wasn't there before, and it serves as a constant reminder of how fragile everything feels now.

Determined to make things better, Jamie speaks up at dinner that night. "I think we need to do something, not just for Lucas, but for everyone. Other kids might be going through the same thing."

His parents exchange a look, and the silence between them says everything.

Finally, his mom nods.

"You're right, Jamie. It's time we step up."

Her words hang in the air like a challenge—a challenge that Jamie can't ignore. But as the evening goes on, the pressure in his chest doesn't let up.

He wants to believe that things will get better, that Lucas will be okay, but there's a nagging thought in the back of his mind: What if it's not over? What if it happens again?

The next day at lunch, Jamie sees Sam. His usually quiet friend is sitting alone on the edge of the playground. Normally, Sam would be out on the field, kicking a ball or laughing with the others. But today, he's hunched over on a bench, picking at his hoodie cuffs.

Jamie hesitates, then walks over.

"Hey, Sam," he says, sitting beside him. "You okay?"

Sam doesn't look up at first. Then, in a voice barely above a whisper, he says,

"It's Kyle. He's been sending me stuff... nasty messages."

Jamie's stomach drops. Kyle. Again. His mind races back to Lucas, to the silence that led to the hospital visit, to the fear, the anxiety. But this time, it's different—Sam's telling someone.

"Did you tell anyone?" Jamie asks, his voice steady but urgent.

Sam nods, his voice shaking.

"Yeah. Miss Taylor this morning. I showed her everything."

Relief floods Jamie's chest, mixing with the anger that's been building. He exhales deeply.

"Good. That was brave, Sam. They'll handle it."

Sam meets his gaze with tired eyes.

"Do you think it'll stop?"

Jamie thinks about Lucas, about all the times they hadn't spoken up, and he nods firmly.

"Yeah, it will. You did the right thing."

Later that afternoon, an announcement goes out: there's going to be a school-wide assembly.

Jamie sits in the hall, his heart pounding as the headteacher steps up to the microphone. She talks about bullying, kindness, how words can hurt more than people realize.

For the first time, Jamie sees the kids around him actually listening.

The next morning, posters are up around the school:

"Speak Up, Stay Safe," and "It's okay not to be okay. Ask for help."

Jamie doesn't see Kyle after the assembly. Whispers fill the hallways, suggesting that his parents were called in, and the school is keeping an eye on him now.

Jamie knows that won't undo what happened, but it's a start.

That evening, as Jamie watches his parents clear the dishes, his dad ruffles his hair as he passes by. A rare smile tugs at his lips.

"Proud of you, son," his dad says. "You're making a difference."

Jamie isn't sure if that's true yet, but for the first time in weeks, the knot in his chest feels a little looser. He thinks about Sam, about Lucas, and about how things could've been different if they'd spoken up sooner.

Maybe, just maybe, this time things really are changing.

Chapter 7 The Blame Game

Lucas walks across the playground, clutching his bag tightly.

The sun is out, but it doesn't make the knot in his stomach go away. Ever since the assembly, things had felt different—safer, maybe—but not entirely.

He keeps his head down as he heads toward the bench by the fence, a place he's come to think of as his safe spot. He's almost there when a voice stops him in his tracks.

"Oi, Lucas."

Lucas freezes. He knows that voice. Turning slowly, he sees Kyle standing a few feet away, hands shoved into his pockets, his face twisted in a sneer.

"Nice job, loser," Kyle says. "Now everyone thinks they can grass on me because of you. This is your fault. Think you're some kind of hero, huh?"

Lucas feels his heart race, his palms slick with sweat.

"I... I didn't—" he starts, but Kyle cuts him off.

"Don't lie!" Kyle snaps, stepping closer. "Because of you, Sam went running to a teacher. Now I'm in trouble, and everyone thinks I'm the bad guy. This isn't over."

Lucas wants to run, but his legs won't move. Kyle's words hit him hard, making him question everything. What if I made things worse? Maybe I shouldn't have said anything.

Kyle leans in, his voice low. "You think you're safe now? You've got no idea what you've done."

Jamie Steps In

"Back off, Kyle."

Both boys turn.

Jamie is standing a few feet away, his hands clenched into fists, his face serious. He doesn't look scared, just angry.

Kyle snorts.

"What are you gonna do about it? You're just a little kid."

Jamie marches closer, his voice steady.

"Leave him alone. You're just picking on him because you're a bully."

Kyle glares at him.

"This isn't your problem. Stay out of it."

Jamie shakes his head.

"Yeah, it is my problem. He's my friend."

For a moment, Kyle looks like he's about to shove Jamie, but then a teacher's voice calls out across the playground, sharp and commanding. Kyle steps back, scowling.

"This isn't over," he mutters before turning and walking away.

Lucas sinks onto the bench, his hands shaking.

Jamie sits down beside him, his voice steady but quiet.

"You okay?"

Lucas nods, but he doesn't feel okay.

"What if he's right? What if I just made things worse?"

"You didn't," Jamie says firmly. "You did the right thing. Kyle's just mad because he got caught."

Lucas glances at Jamie, searching his face for reassurance.

"You really think so?"

Jamie nods.

"Yeah. And you're not on your own anymore. We'll tell Miss Taylor what happened, and she'll sort it."

Lucas takes a deep breath, the knot in his stomach loosening just a little. For the first time, he feels like maybe he's not fighting this battle by himself.

Across the playground, Kyle watches them. His face is unreadable, but his eyes are dark and focused.

Lucas feels Jamie's hand on his shoulder and looks away.

Maybe things really are changing, he thinks. But it's not over yet.

Chapter 8
Whispers of Courage

The bell rings, signalling the end of the school day, but Lucas can't shake the feeling that something has changed. It's as if the world around him is moving faster, yet he's standing still. Every step he takes feels heavier than it should, every glance from his classmates feels loaded with meaning. But there's a flicker inside him, a spark of courage that wasn't there before.

Jamie walks beside him, hands stuffed in his jacket pockets, eyes ahead.

"You good?" he asks quietly.

"I think so," Lucas replies, his voice hesitant but gaining strength with each word. "It's just... I never thought it would feel like this. Like I actually did something."

"You did," Jamie says with a firm nod. "You spoke up. You're not alone in this anymore."

As they walk through the gates of the school, Lucas notices something he hadn't before. The air feels different, almost electric, like there's a shift happening all around them. Kids are talking, laughing, and some even glance at him. It's subtle, but Lucas can feel the change in the way they look at him now—not with judgment or pity, but with something closer to respect.

And then, he hears it.

"Hey, Lucas," someone calls out.

It's Sam, his quiet friend from the playground, who used to sit alone, eyes always on the ground.

Lucas stops.

"Hey, Sam. You good?"

Sam looks up, his face softer than it was the last time they spoke, but his eyes are still guarded.

"Yeah, I'm okay. You, though? You're different, man."

Lucas raises an eyebrow.

"Different?"

Sam nods, a faint smile tugging at the corners of his mouth.

"Yeah, you stood up to Kyle. And you got the whole school talking."

Lucas isn't sure what to say to that. Part of him feels proud, but the other part wonders if maybe he's just been a part in a game he doesn't fully understand. Still, Sam's words sit heavy in his chest, and for the first time, he feels like his voice matters.

"I didn't mean for it to go this far," Lucas admits. "I just... I couldn't keep quiet anymore."

Sam takes a step closer.

"But you did the right thing. You've got courage, Lucas. I think we all need a little bit of that."

The wind picks up, rustling the leaves on the trees above them, and for a moment, Lucas lets himself believe it. He does have courage. Maybe, just maybe, this is the beginning of something bigger than he could have imagined.

As he turns to leave, Jamie claps him on the back.

"It's gonna be alright, you know. Things are changing."

Lucas nods, his heart racing but his head clearer than before. "Yeah, I think so."

Later that evening, Lucas sits in his room, the quiet of the house feeling heavy. He picks up his phone, his fingers hesitating over the screen as he thinks about what to say. He knows he needs to tell his parents what happened, but he's not sure how.

Finally, he types something simple: Can I talk to you?

He puts the phone down, waiting. His mind races, but his hands feel cold. He knows his parents love him, but part of him is still scared.

He's never told them everything before. He wonders if they'll be upset, or if they'll be disappointed in him.

A few moments later, the phone buzzes with a message.

"We're here, son. What's on your mind? "

Lucas takes a deep breath. It's a start, he thinks.

He isn't sure what he'll say next, but for the first time, it feels like he might finally be able to talk about it. And with that, he feels a quiet strength beginning to settle in. For the first time in a long while, he isn't running from what happened. He isn't hiding in fear. Instead, he's standing tall, ready to face the truth, no matter how hard it is.

He feels something shift within him—a whisper of courage that will carry him forward.

Chapter 9
Echoes of Hurt

A couple of days after the weekend, something shifts at school. The whispers in the hallways, the sneers in the lunchroom—Kyle can feel the tension thickening. It's like the world has suddenly turned its back on him, and he's no longer the one holding the power.

Instead of standing tall, Kyle finds himself shrinking. He's used to being the one to push others down, but now, for the first time, it's happening to him.

Kids who've once been his victims start to stand up to him, no longer afraid to challenge his presence.

The jabs, the insults—they come from all angles now. He hears laughter behind him, and when he turns around, it's not the kind of laughter that once made him feel superior. This time, it's mocking. The tables are turning.

As Kyle walks past the school's terrapins, he spots someone out of the corner of his eye.

His heart sinks when he sees one of the kids, a kid he's tormented for years, standing tall, a look of defiance on their face. The look says it all. He's no longer the king of the playground. For the first time, it feels different.

The power has shifted

But Kyle can't let this happen. He tries to put on a brave face, to stand his ground, but the pressure is mounting. The messages keep coming—nasty comments on his phone, his social media accounts flooded with insults. Every notification is a reminder of how far he's fallen.

That's when he hears it. A small sniffle, barely noticeable, but enough to stop him in his tracks.

Kyle freezes. He turns, his eyes scanning the yard, looking for the source of the sound. Behind the terrapins, just beyond the garden path, he sees the kid—head lowered, hunched over, trying to hide.

The same kid who used to take his punches is now curled up, a tear-streaked face barely visible through the leaves. The air around him is charged with an awkward silence, broken only by the soft sounds of quiet sobs.

For a moment, Kyle feels the sting of reality—this is what he's become; the one who once made others feel small is now the one who feels small.

As Kyle stands there, uncertain of what to do, the others start to gather around. They don't jeer anymore. The teasing has turned to concern, and for the first time, Kyle feels the weight of all the hurt he's caused come crashing down on him.

Then, someone speaks. A voice, soft but firm, from one of the kids he's tormented for years:

"Hey, Kyle. You okay?"

Kyle doesn't answer. Instead, he looks down, refusing to meet their gaze. The shame is too much to bear. This isn't the way it was supposed to go. He wasn't supposed to feel this way.

The whispers start again, but this time, they're not about his strength. They're about him. People are talking—not about his strength, his toughness, but about the kid who's been hiding behind the terrapins, unable to hold it together. A hand reaches out, offering help—not a punch, not a taunt, but an invitation to be something more than the bully he's been.

Kyle freezes, the offer hanging in the air like a challenge he's not ready to face. His heart pounds as he watches the hand, the soft but firm gesture of kindness, and his instinct is to pull away. His pride, the very thing that's kept him afloat all these years, tightens in his chest.

"Who does this kid think he is? "Kyle thinks bitterly. "You think you can just fix me? "

The whispers keep coming, each word feeling like a strike against him, but now they're not about him—they're about what he's become.

He can hear them—loser, weak, pathetic—echoing around him, a reminder of how quickly he's fallen from the top.

A cold sweat breaks out on his neck. This wasn't how it was supposed to be. He was supposed to be in control. He was supposed to be feared. But now I'm the one hiding. His mind races as he stands there, torn between the image he's worked so hard to maintain and the truth staring him in the face.

He looks down at the hand again, and something inside him cracks. His ego flares up, his pride a shield to protect him from the vulnerability threatening to engulf him.

"Don't let them see you like this. "Kyle's mind whispers. "You're strong. You can handle this. Don't let them see your weakness. "

For a moment, he considers walking away, pretending like he didn't see it, like he doesn't feel the sting of their eyes on him. But then his chest tightens, and the words come out before he can stop them.

"I don't need your help," Kyle spits, his voice hoarse, but loud enough to push back the silence. "I'm not some little kid."

The false pride clubbed with the shame rises in him, the ego mixing with the anger, the fear, the humiliation.

He can feel the old instincts coming back—the need to fight, to lash out. He turns his back on the hand, the offer, the kindness.

He steps forward, but his steps falter as his thoughts spiral.

"What am I doing? This isn't who I'm supposed to be. I'm supposed to be the one in control. The one everyone looks up to in fear. But the walls are closing in. I can't breathe. The pressure, the weight of all the things I've done, is suffocating me.

Then, as if on cue, a voice interrupts the growing chaos in his head.

"You don't have to do this alone, you know; it's ok not to be okay."

Kyle's heart skips a beat. He knows the voice. He knows it's not an enemy. It's not someone he can push down, someone he can bully into silence. It's... someone who's reaching out.

But pride refuses to let him accept the offer. His fists clench by his sides, his throat tight with unshed tears he doesn't want anyone to see.

He's supposed to be tough. He's supposed to be unbreakable. But standing there, faced with the kindness and the truth of his own actions, Kyle realizes the real battle isn't with those around him. It's with himself.

He can't escape it. He can't outrun it anymore. For the first time, he feels what it's like to be truly alone.

The whispers inside his head grow louder, drowning out everything around him. He can feel the walls closing in—his shoulders stiff, his chest tight. He wants to scream, but the words get caught in his throat.

He's not sure if it's because he's afraid to show weakness or because he's afraid to admit the truth.

"I'm alone, "Kyle thinks, clenching his fists. "I'm not the big guy anymore. I'm the one people talk about behind my back. If they only knew. "

The shame grows heavier with every step he takes away from the hand, away from the kindness that was offered. But as he walks, he feels it—the crushing weight of everything he's done.

His thoughts spiral back to the hurtful words he's said to others, the taunts and the cruelty he's spread.

All the things he's done, the way he's made people feel small. All of it was supposed to make him feel powerful, but now... now it just feels empty.

He rounds the corner of the school, trying to push the guilt and shame away, but it lingers. It gnaws at him. The images of his past, the memories of the kids he's hurt, come crashing down like waves, and he realizes something:

"They weren't afraid of me. They were afraid of the things I was too scared to face. "

The realization hits him harder than anything else. His fists unclench as the weight of his actions sinks in. He feels like an imposter—a person who's been pretending to be something he's not for so long, and now it's too late to take it all back.

He isn't the powerful bully. He's the scared kid hiding behind a fake exterior, afraid of everything—afraid of being seen for who he really is. A victim too. A victim in desperate need of help, but too proud to ask for it.

And just like that, Kyle stops in his tracks. He stands still, his heart pounding in his chest, as he realizes—he's not the bully he thought he was. He's the bullied. He's the one who's been scared for so long, hiding behind anger, behind the masks he's created for himself. But even as that truth settles in, he feels something deeper—the gnawing fear of not knowing what comes next.

Where does he go from here?

"Can I really change? "

However, the shame and fear take over and tighten around his chest, making it feel hard to breathe.

Chapter 10 Threads of Truth

The next day, the whispers started again. Not about Kyle's bravado, not about his power, but about the space he'd left behind.

Kyle hadn't been at school for two days. A lot of kids noticed. They always noticed when someone was missing, especially someone like Kyle—someone who usually cause a stir, who'd either made people laugh or made them cringe. But now there was only silence where there had been laughter or fear.

"Have you seen Kyle lately?" Jamie asked Lucas at lunch, the question hanging in the air like a cloud.

Lucas shook his head. "No. I thought he'd be here today. He wasn't even in class yesterday."

"Maybe he's just sick," Jamie suggested, but there was doubt in his voice.

There was something in the air, an undercurrent of worry that the school couldn't ignore. It wasn't just that Kyle wasn't there. It was the way things had shifted, the strange silence where once there was tension.

After lunch, the bell rang and the halls filled with the usual noise of students heading to their next class. But in the staff room, the teachers were talking in hushed tones. Whispers of something wasn't right. Something was wrong.

The news had already begun to spread—Kyle had been absent for two days now. Not a word. No explanation. It was unusual.

And then the door opened.

Two officers entered, their uniforms a stark contrast to the familiar school setting. They asked to speak with the headteacher, and within moments, they were in her office, asking questions. Quiet at first, then more pointed.

They wanted to know about Kyle—about his behaviour, his friends, his relationships with others at school. What was going on? Was there any indication something might have been wrong?

One of the officers glanced at the headteacher, his eyes scanning the room.

"Has there been anything...untoward? Any bullying? Any signs of distress?"

The question hung heavy in the room, and for a moment, there was nothing but silence.

The headteacher shifted in her seat, her face pinched in thought.

"There has been some recent tension, but nothing major. At least not that I'm aware of," she replied.

Her voice was steady, but her eyes betrayed her—she was worried.

The officers exchanged looks and nodded. It was clear they had heard things. Things that didn't add up. But before they could ask more questions, the bell rang for the end of the school day.

The Questions That Won't Stop

By the time Jamie and Lucas walked home that afternoon, the police had already asked both of them questions. They were calm, professional, but their questions dug deeper than expected. They wanted to know about Kyle. Did they know if he was feeling alright? Had he been acting strange? Was there anything they knew about his home life? The questions were hard to answer. They weren't about to tell the police about the things Kyle had done to them, not without fully understanding the consequences.

"Has anyone heard from him?" Lucas asked, looking at Jamie as they walked.

"No," Jamie replied, a frown deepening on his face. "But I don't know if I care anymore. Because he's been... he's been horrible."

"I don't know," Lucas murmured. "Something feels weird. I don't know why, but I don't want to see him get hurt."

"Why?"

Lucas paused, looking away.

"Because... it's not about what he did to us. It's about what happened to make him that way. Don't you think?"

Jamie stared at him, blinking. He hadn't really thought about it that way before because it's not usually the way a young kid thinks, but as the words hung in the air, something clicked. Kyle wasn't just the bully. He was also the victim.

He doesn't deserve if something bad is happening to him, even if he had done terrible things to others.

The Missing Pieces

Two days later, the police were back, and this time, they weren't just asking questions. They had to.

Kyle was officially missing.

The school had received calls from his parents, frantic and worried. They hadn't heard from Kyle since he'd left school on Monday. His phone had gone unanswered. He hadn't come home. And now, a dark weight settled over the school. The authorities were involved, but no one had any answers.

Social services had gotten involved too, not just because of his disappearance, but because of something darker. They had known for some years that Kyle's home life was unstable. They had been tracking his situation, trying to intervene before it was too late.

But the system had failed him. The family had failed him.

And now, Kyle's missing.

Jamie and Lucas sit in the living room that night, staring at the news, waiting for updates, but none came. No one knew where Kyle was. No one knew what had happened to him.

"We have to do something," Jamie said suddenly, the words bursting out of him. "We can't just wait for someone else to fix this. People need to know what happened. Kyle's been hurt. He's hurt everyone, but he's hurting too."

Lucas nodded, his face set. "Maybe we can help somehow. Maybe we just need to talk to the teachers or the police—let them know what we've seen. Maybe it's not too late for him."

For the first time, Jamie didn't argue. Because something in him had shifted too.

Threads of Truth

Threads of truth began to unravel that night, slowly but surely, weaving a pattern of understanding.

Kyle wasn't just a bully. He was a product of his circumstances, the child of a broken home where violence and neglect had shaped him into what he had became.

The story of what had happened to Kyle isn't just about punishment. It was about healing—not for Kyle, who was still lost somewhere in his own turmoil, but for the others, the ones who had carried the weight of his actions, and for the community that needs to understand the true cost of silence.

Chapter 11 Dangerous Echoes

The search for Kyle continues, but the deeper the community digs, the more uncomfortable the answers become.

People start talking—not about his disappearance, but about the truth they've ignored for years.

In the wake of his vanishing, a clearer picture of Kyle's life begins to emerge, one that paints a disturbing portrait of a family in turmoil.

Kyle's Family Background; a Cycle of Emotional Abuse

Kyle's family has always been a topic of whispers, but no one has dared to speak out—until now.

His father, a man of few words, is known in town for his cold, distant nature and an ever-present bottle in his hand. Rumour has it that he too was bullied as a child, a trauma that compounded his rage and bitterness.

By the time Kyle is born, the cycle of abuse is already firmly in place. His father's drinking escalates over the years, and the home Kyle grows up in is filled with violence, neglect, and constant tension.

Kyle's older brother, once a figure of authority in the house, inherits the anger from their father. The bullying starts early. His brother is the first to hurt him—with words, then with fists.

All the while, their father turns a blind eye, unable or unwilling to break the cycle.

Kyle grows up in this toxic environment, conditioned to believe that love is earned through fear, that power is proven by the dominance of rage.

As the town begins to unravel Kyle's past, mental health professionals step in, recognizing the damage done to him as a child.

His father's alcoholism is more than just a vice—it is a contributing factor to Kyle's own mental health issues. His father's inability to cope with his trauma constructively makes him lash out, and Kyle, the youngest, bears the brunt of it.

What Kyle's family never acknowledges is the toll it takes on his psyche. The neglect, the physical abuse, and the emotional isolation create a perfect storm. As Kyle's behaviour grows more erratic, the whispers around town grow louder.

"Was he the bully? Or was he just another victim of a broken system? "

It isn't until Kyle disappears that the cracks in the system become glaringly obvious.

Police interviews with family members reveal the extent of Kyle's family's dysfunction.

His father has faced numerous charges over the years—assaults, alcohol-related offenses, and domestic abuse—but has always slipped through the cracks.

Mental health professionals have long tried to intervene, but the stigma surrounding mental illness in their community has always kept them at bay.

Even when criminal convictions are brought against Kyle's father, they have never truly stuck.

A cycle of violence that has been ignored for too long has left irreversible scars.

Now, Kyle's situation is the most recent—and perhaps the most tragic—consequence of negligence. The emotional damage, the cycle of bullying, and the lack of support have created many victims—but not in the way that most believe .

As Kyle's story unfolds, it becomes clear that no one is entirely innocent.

Yes, Kyle has been a bully, but he is also a victim—of abuse, neglect, and an emotional void too large to ignore. He has never learned to process his feelings, never had the chance to break free from the patterns set by his family.

Though the world has only seen his anger and violence, the truth is far more complicated.

The community now faces the difficult truth: Kyle has been the product of an environment that fostered his pain. The whispers of his past are no longer just about his actions; they are about the life he has led.

The police, social services, and even the school begin to wonder if healing is possible—not just for Kyle, but for his family as a whole.

Could someone like Kyle ever change? Could the cycle of abuse, fear, and neglect ever be broken? And could his disappearance somehow open the door to a larger conversation about mental health and support for those who have suffered in silence?

The law has its role in ensuring accountability, but mental health professionals know that healing can't come from legal action alone.

The scars run deep, and with Kyle's disappearance, many wonder if the real fight is just beginning.

Could the cycle be broken? Can a community so entrenched in silence and fear ever truly heal?

Chapter 12
The Next Battle

Kyle's disappearance has left the town in a haze of confusion, the answers remaining just out of reach. It's been days, but the silence is growing louder.

No one knows where he is, but the rumours start to spread quickly. Some say he's run away to London, like so many kids his age decide when they want to escape everything.

The city, they say, is where you go to disappear.

People whisper it in the halls, on the streets, under their breath.

It's the only explanation anyone can hold on to—a kid like Kyle, with his hardened exterior, trying to escape his broken home, his complicated past. But even the whispers don't make sense.

Kyle wouldn't have left. Not like that.

Lucas and Jamie are no different from the others; they hear the rumours, too.

The words echo in their minds, bouncing around like a ball they can't catch. Run away to London? It doesn't sit right with them. They know Kyle too well. They know the fear he carries, the bravado he hides behind, the weight of everything he's endured.

London doesn't sound like freedom. It sounds like a place to bury your troubles, to drown in them. Yet, there's no proof. Just speculation. Just voices.

The next few days feel like a blur, the days stretching longer with every unanswered question.

The town keeps going, life moves on, but something feels permanently broken.

And with each passing day, the questions grow:

Where is Kyle? Why hasn't he come back? Has someone taken him. Or worse still, has someone hurt him?

Chapter 13 Lessons in Shadows

The next morning, the tension in the air at school is palpable. Whispers fly as soon as the bell rings, not about tests or homework, but about Kyle. His disappearance is no longer just a local tragedy—it's a mystery with growing uncertainty.

Rumours spread faster than the truth ever could.

Some say Kyle has run away to London, a place where kids his age sometimes vanish to escape their lives. But the truth? No one knows.

As the day wears on, it becomes clear that something has changed. A female police officer—a support officer, dressed in a dark jacket and pants—arrives at school, accompanied by a social worker. They speak briefly with the headteacher before heading down the halls.

The whispers intensify. Lucas and Jamie are both summoned to the office after lunch.

Their parents are already waiting, and when they enter, the weight of the situation is clear.

There is no explanation for why they are being questioned, but the presence of the officer and the social worker makes it clear: this isn't just a casual conversation.

"Lucas," the officer says, her tone firm but not unkind. "We need to ask you a few questions about Kyle. It's just routine, but you're being questioned under caution. Your parents are here for support."

Jamie exchanges a nervous glance with Lucas, but his friend says nothing, just nodding slightly. It feels strange—being questioned like this. He has never imagined that helping Kyle would lead to something like this.

The officer looks at Jamie now.

"Jamie, we'll be asking you a few questions as well. You're both connected to this case, and we need to be sure we get all the information we can. Please don't be worried; you're not in any trouble. We're just following procedure."

Lucas swallows hard, feeling a cold lump form in his throat. He thinks back to the times Kyle has picked on him, the insults, the threats, the pushes in the hallways. But all that seems distant now, like a world far removed from this moment. He isn't sure what will happen next, but he doesn't want to make things worse.

Once they are led to separate rooms, the questions begin. At first, they ask about Kyle—his behaviour, his history with the two boys. It feels like the longest hour of Lucas' life, his mind racing for the right answers, trying not to say anything that will make things worse.

"What do you think happened to Kyle?" the social worker asks softly, but it feels sharp, as if the question itself could cut through him.

"I... I don't know," Lucas mutters. "He just... he just disappeared." They ask the same questions over and over, probing, trying to make sense of things that don't make sense. How did Kyle go from the bully to the missing kid? Why hadn't anyone seen it coming?

After what seems like forever, they are finally allowed to leave. As the officer and social worker exchange quiet words, Lucas and Jamie sit together in the hallway, staring at the floor.

"Well, that was... weird," Jamie says, trying to lighten the mood, though his voice is tight. "I'm just glad it's over."

"Yeah," Lucas replies, still dazed. "But... what if they find out something we didn't know?"

Jamie frowns. "What do you mean?"

Lucas doesn't answer right away. His mind is still racing.

The police are right to ask questions. After all, they are both the last ones who had seen Kyle. But he can't shake the feeling that something is wrong—something has gone terribly wrong, and Kyle's disappearance is just the beginning.

As they step outside, the weight of everything that's happened presses down on them, but it's not over. It can't be.

What happens next will change everything for Kyle, for them, and for everyone who's been part of this story. The truth is still out there, waiting to be uncovered.

But for now, the silence remains, heavy with the weight of unanswered questions.

Chapter 14
A New Chapter Begins

The school is buzzing with whispers—quiet at first, but growing louder with every passing hour. Kyle has been missing for weeks, and the uncertainty has hung over the school like a heavy fog.

However, today, something's different. The rumours start small, shared between a few students in hushed voices.

"Did you hear? They think they found him. Kyle's back."

Some shake their heads, not believing it, but the whispers keep growing, spreading like wildfire through the halls. No one knows where the news has come from, but the uncertainty in the air is palpable.

Is it true? Is Kyle really back?

It's lunchtime when the rumour reaches Jamie and Lucas. They're sitting in the cafeteria, picking at their food, but their minds are elsewhere.

The past few weeks have been filled with questions and silence, the kind of silence that fills up the space between friends. But now, with every passing moment, they feel the weight of the rumour pressing in.

Jamie's phone buzzes. He picks it up, scrolling through the message.

"Kyle's been found. He's safe, but nobody knows where he's been."

They exchange a glance, a flicker of disbelief passing between them. Could it really be true?

"Where has he been?" Lucas mutters, his voice low, full of confusion. "How could he just disappear like that?"

The question hangs in the air as the bell rings, and the two boys walk to their next class in silence.

As they pass the hallways, they see more students gathered, talking, their faces a mixture of relief and confusion. It's clear that no one really knows what's happening.

Later, a female police officer and a social worker show up at the school. They don't come with answers. Instead, they bring a storm of new questions.

The staff and parents are told that Kyle might be back. Or he might not be. No one knows yet. The uncertainty stretches into the night, and the next day, the whispers reach a crescendo. Kyle's been found.

But no one can say where he's been, or why he left. There's still so much unknown.

The only thing everyone can agree on is that things are different now.

Kyle is no longer the face of the bully. But the question remains—what happened to him? Why did he leave? And more importantly, what will happen now?

Kyle's return—if it is truly him—is a turning point. But for the school, for Lucas and Jamie, the real question isn't about what happened to Kyle.

It's about what happens next.

Chapter 15
Picking Up The Pieces

Kyle stands at the edge of the playground, his eyes cast downward, not meeting anyone's gaze.

Kyle should've been long gone from junior school by now, moving on to secondary like the rest of his mates. But no—he was still here, a twelve-year-old stuck with kids a year younger. Being held back was something his family never let him forget.

At home, it was relentless. His dad would roll his eyes every time Kyle didn't know the answer to something, muttering,

"What do they even teach you in that school?"

His mum wasn't much better, muttering about how it

"He's a slow learner." to the neighbours.

His older brother, though, was the worst. He'd call him "thick" or "slow" at every opportunity, throwing out insults like darts, each one sticking a little deeper.

Initially, Kyle made sure no one else got the chance to call him names. He learned quickly that being the bully gave him power, gave him control. If he threw the first punch, he didn't have to feel the weight of anyone else's words.

"Did you hear?" one of the teachers had said in hushed tones during lunch duty. "Kyle's been seen; he's back. "

For weeks, he had been missing—lost in a maze of confusion and fear. His return is met with whispers, but the truth about where he went doesn't matter. The rumours of London, the idea of running away to escape, no longer have the power they once did. Because Kyle knows now, more than ever, running only made things worse.

In the silence that surrounds him, he's beginning to understand something he couldn't see before.

His pride, his fear, and the anger that kept him hiding behind walls have only isolated him further. For so long, he believed that staying silent was the only way to protect himself.

He thought that pretending to be strong, pretending to be unbreakable, would save him from the vulnerability he couldn't bear to face. But it didn't. It only kept him trapped in the dark, where no one could reach him, and no one could understand.

Now, standing here, the truth is starting to pierce through the walls he's built around himself. He should have asked for help. He should have reached out, not just for himself, but for the ones he hurt along the way. The people who might have understood, who might have offered the help he needed.

But by staying silent, by holding onto his pride, Kyle let things spiral further than he could ever imagine. He let the pain grow until it was all-consuming, and he thought running away would solve it.

But now, as the pieces of his life start to fall back into place, he understands that running away doesn't solve anything. It only delays the inevitable.

What serves your life is not running from the truth, but facing it head-on. What serves your life is asking for help when you need it.

What serves your life is letting go of the ego and embracing the fact that you are not alone.

Lucas watches Kyle from a distance. He knows the struggle Kyle is going through. They've both been caught in the same cycle of fear, of hurt, and of silence. But now, Kyle has begun to break free. It's not easy. It's not quick. But it's a start. A small step in the right direction.

Jamie walks up next to Lucas, the weight of the moment heavy on his shoulders. He doesn't say anything, just nods toward Kyle.

There's an understanding in the air, a quiet realization that Kyle is no longer the bully. He's the one who needs help, and he's finally beginning to ask for it.

This is what happens when we let go of the false armour we wear, the masks we create to shield ourselves from the world.

Kyle, for the first time, sees that the real strength comes from vulnerability. It comes from saying, "I need help," from letting someone else see the pain we've been hiding for so long.

The whispers around him are no longer about his strength, but about the courage it takes to admit you're not okay. To admit you need help.

Kyle knows now—he can't fix everything alone. And he doesn't have to. There are people who want to help. People who understand. People who can show him that it's okay to fall, but it's even more important to get back up.

Kyle looks around the playground, and for the first time, he doesn't feel so alone.

He knows that this isn't the end of the road. It's the beginning of something new.

Although be it a long journey toward healing. It won't necessarily be easy. It's not instant. But it's real.

And in that moment, he makes a silent promise to himself—he will never run away again.

He will face whatever comes next. Because the true strength lies in asking for help, in breaking the silence, and in understanding that no matter how hard things get, there is always hope.

Chapter 16 Turning The Table

As the story in the book ends, a young boys dad gently closes the book about Lucas & the bully, the sound soft in the quiet living room.

The lad who's name is Michael sits across from his father, his eyes fixed on the book, his fingers twisting nervously in his lap.

"Are you okay, son?" his dad asks, his voice calm and caring.

Michael shrugs, his gaze not lifting. "Yeah, I'm fine," he mumbles, though the weight in his tone says otherwise.

His dad leans forward slightly, holding the book in his lap. "You know, it's okay not to be okay. Sometimes stories like this can make us think about things we don't want to talk about, and that's alright."

Michael glances up for a moment, his eyes glistening, before quickly looking down again. "Lucas... he didn't look all that scared, did he? Like, when Kyle was being mean to him?"

His father nods gently. "I'm sure he was. But what mattered was that Lucas had people who cared about him, people who wanted to help him."

Michael hesitates, his lip trembling slightly. Then, in a voice barely above a whisper, he says, "There's a Kyle at my school. He's not nice to me either. Calls me names. Sometimes worse than what happened to Lucas."

His dad places the book aside, leaning in closer. "Thank you for telling me, son. I know that wasn't easy. But you did the right thing, and now we can figure out how to make it stop."

Moral of the Story:

1. Awareness Leads to Action: By creating awareness, children feel empowered to speak up.

2. Parents Are Key: The story emphasizes how vital it is for parents to notice, listen, and act.

3. Prevention and Support: The boy doesn't end up in hospital because his parents supported him early on, and the awareness made all the difference.

Chapter 17
The Message: Universal

This story isn't just for children. It isn't even just for parents. It's for every single person who plays a role in the life of a child: the teachers who see them every day, the social workers who step in when things go wrong, the police officers who protect, the health professionals who nurture, and the communities who shape their world.

It's for anyone who believes that children deserve to grow up in a world that understands their struggles, listens to their voices, and stands up for their safety. Because bullying—whether online or in person—doesn't just harm one child. Its ripple effects touch families, schools, and communities.

Why Awareness Matters

Awareness is the first step toward change. Without understanding the problem, we can't begin to fix it. Cyberbullying is silent. It doesn't leave visible bruises, but it leaves scars—deep ones that can shape a child's sense of self-worth and safety.

When we dismiss bullying as "kids being kids," we fail them. When we ignore subtle signs of distress, we allow the cycle to continue.

Awareness means seeing, listening, and taking action before it's too late.

What Can We Do?

For Grown-Ups at Home

Listen Without Judgment: Sometimes, children don't open up because they fear being blamed or misunderstood. Create a safe space where they can share without fear.

Ask the Right Questions: If you notice changes in behaviour, gently ask, "Is everything okay? Is something bothering you?" Open-ended questions invite honesty.

Stay Involved: Know what your child is doing online. Familiarize yourself with the apps and platforms they use. This isn't about spying—it's about being informed and present.

For Educators

Create a Culture of Kindness: Schools should be safe havens. Implement anti-bullying programs, hold discussions about empathy, and ensure every student feels seen and valued.

Watch for Signs: Teachers often see what parents don't. Changes in behaviour, unexplained absences, or a sudden drop in performance can all be indicators of distress.

Intervene Early: Don't wait for things to escalate. If you suspect bullying, act immediately by involving parents, counsellors, or school administrators.

For Social Workers and Counsellors'

Be a Bridge: Social workers play a critical role in connecting families with resources. Offer support that empowers parents to help their children.

Advocate for Education: Ensure that families understand the impact of bullying and know how to navigate these challenges. Awareness campaigns can be lifesaving.

Law Enforcement

Understand the Impact: Cyberbullying is a crime that often goes unreported. Treat every case with the seriousness it deserves.

Cyberbullying is a pervasive issue affecting children worldwide, leading to severe emotional distress and, in tragic cases, loss of life. Recognizing its profound impact, various countries have enacted laws to combat cyberbullying and protect vulnerable individuals.

United Kingdom: The UK addresses cyberbullying through several legal frameworks: Protection from Harassment Act 1997: This act criminalizes behaviour amounting to harassment, which can encompass cyberbullying activities.

Malicious Communications Act 1988: It is an offense to send electronic communications that are indecent, grossly offensive, or contain threats, aligning with many cyberbullying behaviours.

Communications Act 2003: Section 127 targets the improper use of public electronic communications networks, including sending offensive or menacing messages.

These laws collectively provide mechanisms to prosecute individuals engaging in cyberbullying. Additionally, the UK government has proposed the Online Safety Bill, aiming to impose a duty of care on online platforms to protect users, especially children, from harmful content.

United States: In the U.S., cyberbullying legislation varies by state: State Laws: Many states have enacted laws addressing cyberbullying, with some incorporating provisions into their education codes, mandating schools to implement anti-bullying policies that cover electronic harassment.

Federal Law: While there isn't a specific federal law targeting cyberbullying, certain actions may fall under federal statutes related to harassment or stalking. The decentralized approach results in varying degrees of protection and enforcement across the country.

European Union: The EU has taken steps to address cyberbullying among member states: Framework Agreement on Harassment and Violence at Work (2007): This agreement aims to prevent harassment, including cyberbullying, in the workplace.

However, there is currently no EU-wide legislation specifically targeting cyberbullying among young people. Individual member states have their own laws and policies, leading to a fragmented approach across Europe.

Australia: Australia has implemented comprehensive measures against cyberbullying: Enhancing Online Safety Act 2015: This act established the Office of the Safety Commissioner, which has the authority to investigate and act on complaints about cyberbullying material targeted at Australian children.

Criminal Code Act 1995: Certain provisions criminalize the use of a carriage service to menace, harass, or cause offense, applicable to cyberbullying behaviours.

These legislative measures are complemented by educational programs and resources aimed at prevention and awareness.

Canada: Canada addresses cyberbullying through both federal and provincial laws: Criminal Code: Amendments include offenses related to the non-consensual distribution of intimate images and harassment, which can encompass cyberbullying activities.

Provincial Legislation: Several provinces have enacted laws requiring schools to have anti-bullying policies that address cyberbullying.

These efforts are supported by public awareness campaigns and educational initiatives.

New Zealand: New Zealand has specific legislation targeting harmful digital communications:

Harmful Digital Communications Act 2015: This act aims to deter, prevent, and mitigate harm caused by digital communications and provides avenues for victims to seek redress.

The legislation establishes principles for responsible online behaviour and sets up mechanisms for addressing complaints.

Conclusion: While legislative measures are crucial in combating cyberbullying, they must be complemented by education, awareness, and community engagement to create a safe and supportive environment for children worldwide.

Collaborate with Schools and Families: Build trust with the communities you serve. When children and parents feel supported, they are more likely to come forward.

For Health Professionals

Address Mental Health: Many victims of bullying struggle with anxiety, depression, and other mental health challenges. Offer resources and referrals for ongoing care.

Educate Families: Provide parents with information on how to recognize the signs of emotional distress and where to seek help.

A Message for Grown-Ups

Inclusion is the Answer

This isn't just about one child or one family—it's about all of us. Inclusion means acknowledging that every child matters and that we all share the responsibility of protecting them. It means recognizing that bullying is a societal issue that requires a collective response.

When we come together—as parents, teachers, social workers, police officers, and caring individuals—we create a world where no child feels alone.

What Does Change Look Like?

Change happens when:

A teacher notices a quiet child and reaches out.

A parent takes time to listen, even when life is busy.

A police officer treats a report of bullying with the same care as any other crime.

A community rallies together to say, "This isn't okay."

Change looks like children growing up knowing they are valued, safe, and heard.

Your Role in This Movement

Every one of us has a part to play. Whether you're a parent, a professional, or simply someone who cares, your actions matter. Listen. Speak up. Take bullying seriously. Together, we can break the cycle and ensure that no child suffers in silence.

The message is simple:

It's okay not to be okay

Chapter 18
Resources For Support

Resources For Support

Mental Health Support

Mind (UK) – Support for mental health.

Telephone: 0300 123 3393

Email: info@mind.org.uk

Samaritans – Free, 24/7 helpline for those in distress.

Telephone: 116 123

Email: jo@samaritans.org

Child Safety and Protection

NSPCC (National Society for the Prevention of Cruelty to Children)

Telephone: 0808 800 5000

Childline (for children): 0800 1111

Cyberbullying and Online Safety

Childline – Free help for children.

Telephone: 0800 1111

Internet Matters – Resources for online safety.

Addiction Support

Alcoholics Anonymous (AA)

Telephone: 0800 917 7650

Narcotics Anonymous (NA)

Website:

Telephone: 0300 999 1212

Family Support

Family Lives – Support for parenting and family issues.

Telephone: 0808 800 2222

General Wellbeing

Young Minds – Mental health support for young people and their parents.

Parent helpline: 0808 802 5544

Relate – Counselling for families and relationships.

Telephone: 0300 003 0396

Global Resources:

1. Child Helpline International global network of child helplines that connect children with local services for support.
Website: www.childhelplineinternational.org

2. UNICEF (United Nations Children's Fund)Offers support for children's rights and safety worldwide.
Website: www.unicef.org

3. Stop Bullying.gov While U.S.-focused, it provides globally applicable strategies to deal with bullying and cyberbullying.
Website: www.stopbullying.gov

USA Resources:

1. 988 Suicide & Crisis Life line Free 24/7 support for anyone in mental health distress or crisis.
Phone: 988
Website: www.988lifeline.org

2. Cyberbullying Research CenterDedicated to providing research-based strategies to address cyberbullying.
Website: www.cyberbullying.org

3. National Parent HelplineSupport for parents to navigate challenges their children might face, including cyberbullying.
Phone: 1-855-427-2736
Website: www.nationalparenthelpline.org

Printed in Great Britain
by Amazon

aadf8553-741a-43c6-8bf7-f323124e759cR02